Before You Know It

By:
Martha Dove

Published by Melanin Origins

PO Box 122123; Arlington, TX 76012

All rights reserved, including the right of reproduction in whole

or in part in any form.

Copyright 2022

First Edition

The author asserts the moral right under the Copyright, Designs and Patents Act of 1988 to be identified as the author of this work.

This novel is a work of fiction. The names, characters and incidents portrayed in the work, other than those clearly in the public domain, are of the author's imagination and are not to be construed as real. Any resemblance to actual persons, living or dead, events or localities, is entirely coincidental.

All rights reserved. No part of this publication may be reproduced, stored in a retrieval system or transmitted, in any form by any means without the prior consent of the author, nor be otherwise circulated in any form of binding or cover other than that with which it is published and without a similar condition being imposed on the subsequent purchaser.

Library of Congress Control Number: 2022903061

ISBN: 978-1-62676-389-0 hardback

ISBN: 978-1-62676-437-8 paperback

ISBN: 978-1-62676-057-8 ebook

This book is dedicated to my five beautiful daughters. May you soar and be all that you were created to be. May you know your worth and do far greater than mommy ever did. Love you!!

Hi, I am Little Taylor Olivia and I have something big to say. I love you and I want you to be your best one day. So listen now. Hear me loud and clear! Don't let these words disappear!

They are very important. They will help you in life. You'll have exceeding joy and lots of delight. Remember, life is short and before you know it....

You will need a friend, so try to be a friend. It's not always the easiest thing to do. But I'm sure you'll get the hang of it. Just do as I do. Be nice and care about others.

Be there when your friend needs to talk about something that bothers them or makes them sad. Don't tell their secrets or be rude. That will make them really mad!

When they are sad, tell a few jokes. Be a Silly Willy or a Clowney Brownie, and if all else fails, hug them. Just like me. That seems to work. One day you will need someone to be there for you, so for now, try being there for them.

Before you know it, you will need someone to share with you. So try to share while you have the chance.

Would you like some candy?

I know it may be hard to share your toys or those gummy bears that were just too delicious to let a friend have a taste. But it's good to share. After all, it's better to give than to take.

It makes you feel better because you helped to put a smile on someone's face. One day, you may need someone to share with you. And guess what, they will remember the time you shared and return the favor.

Before you know it, you will be a mom or dad. So listen to your parents while you're a kid. They may not always ask you to do the things you want to do. I know you may want to stay up late to play that one last game....

Watch one last show or read one last book. But mom and dad know what's best, and they love you. They won't do anything to hurt you. You are their greatest joy.

They want you to succeed. It may be hard to see, but try to do what they ask and be the best you can be.

Before you know it, you will be a teacher. So be nice and listen to yours. Be ready to learn when you walk through the door.

You've lost all the good stuff. What a waste! Like you ran and ran but didn't win the race. Loss of focus has cost you first place.

Please don't call her name all day or keep getting out of your seat. They don't like that. It's a pet peeve. Instead, learn what she is teaching because one day you may be in her shoes. And you'll probably ask to be excused.

Mrs. Martin!

Believe it or not, many people look up to you. So don't follow what is wrong. Go the other way! Don't do what others are doing. It will be a big mistake. One that you do not want to make.

One day, you will be called to do something big. So practice, practice, practice while no one is looking. Practice until it is as easy as cupcakes. Stand up and do the right thing. Not only will you be a leader, but you could be someone's hero that saves the day!!

Before you know it, you will look back and wonder, "Why did I do that?" Sometimes we do things we do not mean, like tripping a friend or saying the wrong thing.

It may be all fun and games when it is done. Oh, but the problems that haven't even begun!

Or how I wasn't exactly listening when my teacher was teaching and bombed the quiz or took something that wasn't mine and the principal said it was his.

Ok, enough of the stories, you get the idea. Don't do what you will be sorry for later because one day you will ask the same question I asked myself, "Why did I do that?" Only then it will be too late.

Before you know it, you will be an adult. The clock is ticking away. Time flies like a bird. So enjoy right now while you have the time.

You can run around, laugh, and be carefree.
Jump and shout or climb a big tree. Roll in the sand
and get dirt on your hands. Make every moment count.
Cherish them all! You may not get it yet, but you'll understand.

You don't have to worry. No need to pout or cry... Make a frown or even be shy. You just have to try to enjoy "right now" because it will be harder one day. Like solving a big puzzle! But again, don't worry because you'll figure it out somehow.

Before you know it, you will have a big job to do! You may be a doctor, a lawyer, a teacher, a princess, a prince, a king, a queen... a lion, a tiger...a kangaroo.

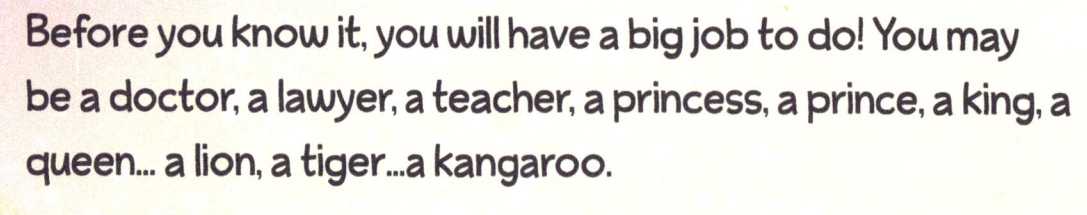

So, learn all the lessons you need to learn. Your future is right around the corner. Success or failure? You can choose it. Tomorrow will be here before you know it!

About the Author

Martha Dove

is an educator, content creator/influencer and woman of faith who aspires to be a great inspiration to everyone she encounters. She was born and raised in the small town of Cofield, North Carolina and had very humble beginnings. She is the wife of Gorden Dove and the mother of 5 beautiful girls; Taylor, Madison, Ava, Noelle and Grace Dove. Her daughters were great inspirations for the writing of this book. It is crucial for Martha to create pathways to allow her children to see themselves in storybooks.

As an educator, she followed in the footsteps of her father (a retired teacher) and has 15 years of experience in shaping the young mind. She holds a bachelor's degree in Elementary Ed and a Masters in Curriculum and instruction. She is also a product of an HBCU (Elizabeth City State University). She was deemed Teacher of the Year for the 2020-2021 school year, yet works diligently to not just obtain titles, but make a lasting impact on the next generation.

As a content creator, she co-founded Doves Nest with her husband, a channel promoting lifestyle, music, inspiration and family. She has also partnered with many national and local brands and loves connecting with her audience.

Her favorite quote is one her father consistently recited during her childhood ~ "Reach for the moon and if you fall amongst the stars, you'll still be on higher ground."~Norman Vincent Peale